Rainbow Remnants

in Rock Bottom

Ghetto Sky

Rainbow Remnants in Rock Bottom Ghetto Sky

THYLIAS MOSS

The National Poetry Series
Selected by Charles Simic

Persea Books
New York

For Eva and Edward

Grateful acknowledgment is made to the following periodicals in which some of the poems in this volume previously appeared: *Best American Poetry 1989, Callaloo, Epoch, Field, Graham House Review, Iris, Pivot, Ploughshares, Pushcart XIV.*

This book was completed with the help of grants from the National Endowment of the Arts and The Kenan Charitable Trust.

For information, address the publisher:
Persea Books
60 Madison Avenue
New York, NY 10010

Library of Congress Cataloging-in-Publication Data

Moss, Thylias.
Rainbow remnants in rock bottom ghetto sky / Thylias Moss.
p.   cm. — (The National poetry series)
ISBN 0-89255-157-7 (paper) : $9.95
I. Title.   II. Series.
PS3563.08856R35   1991
811'.54—dc20   90-23770
                                                      CIP

Set in Garamond by Keystrokes, Lenox, Massachusetts
Printed by Capital City Press, Montpelier, Vermont

First Edition

CONTENTS

I

Renewal at the Pediatric Hospice   3
All Is Not Lost When Dreams Are   5
The Rapture of Dry Ice Burning Off Skin as
    the Moment of the Soul's Apotheosis   6
God Bless Rita's Magic Hair   8
An Anointing   10
While Envying the Amish   12
Tornados   14
Highway 29: A Pedestrian's View   15
The Place That Makes Presidents   17
Detour: The Death of Agnes   19
Dennis's Sky Leopard   22
What Hung Above Our Heads Like Truce   24
Almost an Ode to the West Indian Manatee   26
The Nature of Morning   27
Poem for My Mothers and Other Makers of Asafetida   28

II

Birmingham Brown's Turn   33
Time for Praise   38
The Jonah Effect   40
Special Effects   42
Interpretation of a Poem by Frost   44
The Lynching   45
Preferable Truth   47
The Linoleum Rhumba   49
Green Light and Gamma Ways   51
Miss Liberty Loses Pageant   53
Longing to See a Nurturing Grave   55
News   56
The Warmth of Hot Chocolate   58
Dwarf Tossing   60

III

Congregations   63
Lynne's Poem: Reasons   68

Notes   70

I

RENEWAL AT THE PEDIATRIC HOSPICE

That room that sunlight fully carpets
if you rise at dawn, they all do, seems

full of conjoined children; heads, hands, arms
uniting, at first the strength of numbers but

they are one. They learn the glory of neck
from swans and learn their dive, their song, to

float and know coupling that way, from the reflection
they plan to emancipate like legacy. Each child

is a feather, souvenir of our hoped for,
unearned, ungranted evolution.

I remember them at strange times, shopping, reaching
for instant oatmeal and coffee that spurn delay.

Then in the check-out line with carriage overflowing
I glimpse Garcia's *while-U-wait* repair sign flash

a tribute to the heart's intermittent beat. That's
the best use for the telegraph. I leave through

an automatic door in time to see them paint windows
on their fingernails, make tents with their hair,

fill the whites of their eyes with snow, sculpt
the iris into the pupil's plow that clears

the field of vision for spring in which the whites
become shells and the irises, emerging chicks.

They have X-ray visions, dwindling bone mass, access
to the snowflakes arcing under their skin

where they also wear pulmonary lace
for special, endless nights

on the town when you fall
so deeply in love

you can't get up and everyone
thinks you're dead.

ALL IS NOT LOST WHEN DREAMS ARE

1.

The dreams float like votive lilies
then melt.

It is the way they sing
going down that I envy and to hear it

I could not rescue them. A dirge
reaches my ears like a corkscrew of smoke
And it sits behind my eyes like a piano roll

Some say this is miracle water
None say dreams made it so

2.

Long ago a fish forgot what fins were good for
And flew out of the stream
It was not dreaming
It had no ambition but confusion

In Nova Scotia it lies on ice in the sun
and its eye turns white and pops out like a pearl
when it's broiled

The Titanic is the one that got away.

THE RAPTURE OF DRY ICE BURNING OFF SKIN AS
THE MOMENT OF THE SOUL'S APOTHEOSIS

How will we get used to joy
if we won't hold onto it?

Not even extinction stops me; when
I've sufficient craving, I follow the buffalo,
their hair hanging below their stomachs like
fringes on Tiffany lampshades; they can be turned on
so can I by a stampede, footsteps whose sound
is my heart souped up, doctored, ninety pounds
running off a semi's invincible engine. Buffalo
heaven is Niagara Falls. There their spirit
gushes. There they still stampede and power
the generators that operate the Tiffany lamps
that let us see in some of the dark. Snow
inundates the city bearing their name; buffalo
spirit chips later melt to feed the underground,
the politically dredlocked tendrils of roots. And this
has no place in reality, is trivial juxtaposed with

the faces of addicts, their eyes practically as sunken
as extinction, gray ripples like hurdlers' track lanes
under them, pupils like just more needle sites.
And their arms: flesh trying for a moon apprenticeship,
a celestial antibody. Every time I use it
the umbrella is turned inside out,
metal veins, totally hardened arteries and survival
without anything flowing within, nothing saying
life came from the sea, from anywhere but coincidence
or God's ulcer, revealed. Yet also, inside out
the umbrella tries to be a bouquet, or at least
the rugged wrapping for one that must endure much,
without dispensing coherent parcels of scent,
before the refuge of vase in a room already accustomed
to withering mind and retreating skin. But the smell

of the flowers lifts the corners of the mouth as if
the man at the center of this remorse has lifted her
in a waltz. This is as true as sickness. The Jehovah's

Witness will come to my door any minute with tracts, an
inflexible agenda and I won't let him in because
I'm painting a rosy picture with only blue and
yellow (sadness and cowardice).
I'm something of an alchemist. Extinct.
He would tell me time is running out.
I would correct him: time *ran* out; that's why
history repeats itself, why we can't advance.
What joy will come has to be here right now: Cheer
to wash the dirt away, Twenty Mule Team Borax and
Arm & Hammer to magnify Cheer's power, lemon-scented
bleach and ammonia to trick the nose, improved—changed—
Tide, almost all-purpose starch that cures any limpness
except impotence. Celebrate that there's *Master*card
to rule us, bring us to our knees, the protocol we follow
in the presence of the head of our state of ruin, the
official with us all the time, not inaccessible in
palaces or White Houses or Kremlins. Besides every
ritual is stylized, has patterns and repetitions
suitable for adaptation to dance. Here come toe shoes,
brushstrokes, oxymorons. Joy

is at our tongue tips: let the great thirsts and hungers
of the world be the *marvelous* thirsts, *glorious* hungers.
Let hearbreak be alternative to coffeebreak, five
midmorning minutes devoted to emotion.

GOD BLESS RITA'S MAGIC HAIR

for Rita and Lewis

She said her hair grew only in Arizona
as if all the tricks about living
had nothing to do with all the chalky
cravings, the Milk of Magnesia binges
that helped her mother's body carry Rita.
The Akron dirt was not right, not palatable
or sustaining.

All of a sudden, here was this
Arizonan variety of rain coming down and
in it a net to catch things by their
gills with bobby pin bait. Fishing pole,
tail end of a rat-tail comb, chalked like
a cue stick before entering crinkled, dark
as Boston Harbor water from the scalp shore,
itself a clay place. And appetizing.

The Greyhounds running coast to coast through
every dinky town with pick-up truck or barefoot
connection to every boondock and backwood,
Hazzard and Crawdad Junction, Hatshepsut
Trailer Park, my ancestral places; the bus bellies
crammed with shoeboxes of the dirt (as if for
midget vampires) and fried hard buffalo wings
not indigenous to the north pre-occupied
with other climates and profits and
aberrations. This happened when Virginia
was pregnant with my husband; took the clay she
ate, hand-carried to Peoria by Jasper, into
those invisible hands (for which the ribs
were a kind of octopusine model) inside the body
and sculpted the baby she wanted to have, her
favorite of the nine because he was the one that
made her something besides mother: artist and

happy. There are women—I want to spend this
whole night in devotion to them—who will venture just
for you into the special places with augers, mattocks,
chisels and hoes that broke the ground for the hootenanny
platform and honky tonk foundation; all along
the Mississippi and inland following instinct that
flows the same. They will go by slim creeks, their
calves are wider, mosquitos directly over them like
expirations of factory breath, not the pure,
crystalline breathing of Greenland winter; to roadside
monoliths where interstates cut through hillocks and
mountains exposing edible rock, meteroritic manna; to the
edges of fields sharing a border with desire, and there
they will quarry, cut the wedges and chunks and send them
to you anywhere in the world after they kiss them, the
taste on their lips longer than love, than Rita's magic hair.

AN ANOINTING

Boys have to slash their fingers to become brothers. Girls trade their Kotex, me and Molly do in the mall's public facility.

Me and Molly never remember each other's birthdays. On purpose. We don't like scores of any kind. We don't wear watches or weigh ourselves.

Me and Molly have tasted beer. We drank our shampoo. We went to the doctor together and lifted our specimen cups in a toast. We didn't drink that stuff. We just gargled.

When me and Molly get the urge, we are careful to put it back exactly as we found it. It looks untouched.

Between the two of us, me and Molly have 20/20 vision.

Me and Molly are in eighth grade for good. We like it there. We adore the view. We looked both ways and decided not to cross the street. Others who'd been to the other side didn't return. It was a trap.

Me and Molly don't double date. We don't multiply anything. We don't know our multiplication tables from a coffee table. We'll never be decent waitresses, indecent ones maybe.

Me and Molly do not believe in going ape or going bananas or going Dutch. We go as who we are. We go as what we are.

Me and Molly have wiped each other's asses with ferns. Made emergency tampons of our fingers. Me and Molly made do with what we have.

Me and Molly are in love with wiping the blackboard with each other's hair. The chalk gives me and Molly an idea of what old age is like; it is dusty and makes us sneeze. We are allergic to it.

Me and Molly, that's M and M, melt in your mouth.

What are we doing in your mouth? Me and Molly bet you'll never guess. Not in a million years. We plan to be around that long. Together that long. Even if we must freeze the moment and treat the photograph like the real thing.

Me and Molly don't care what people think. We're just glad that they do.

Me and Molly lick the dew off the morning grasses but taste no honey till we lick each other's tongues.

We wear full maternity sails. We boat upon my broken water. The katabatic action begins, Molly down my canal binnacle first, her water breaking in me like an anointing.

WHILE ENVYING THE AMISH

Expect an early morning unsolicited kiss when
the man beside me wakes with mortality on
his breath though the last thing he recalls eating
is too yeasty bread made while envying the Amish; it
was their turn, everything I envy at least once.

He wakes, kisses me awake, I tasting the salt the way
I did all the time while adjusting to pregnancy though
by the time I did, it was over, confinement—as those
in my mother's day could call it although she didn't—
was over. All the photographs of her show her pregnant

as if that were her career, as if I, her only child annually
passed through the Mecca of her body, a Genesis and Revelation,
my mother resorting to the only complete book in order to
understand fullness. I don't mind walking this road again,
really I'm glad to fit into her again and again as the years

crochet her skin into what is pulled over me every night while
I sleep giving sight and judgment a rest, a chance to recover.
Then also is the praying done, my mother again in her afghan form
puckering into a tent from which the sinful larva emerges redeemed
in the morning, wings and all. Time can always be the culprit; it

keeps running away, red and seconded-handed, never caught, never
it in Hide and Seek. Now I am envying childhood if that is where
imaginary embraces are felt like real ones, imaginary monsters
try to bite but their teeth fall out and imaginary fish
use them as replacement fins and the fish scales rain down

in the kitchen like the guts of a piñata swinging like a
pendulum the child breaks and stops time, whose teeth just
wouldn't fall, from ever hurting us again. Now I envy
the daughters (well, sons too) of doctors; death put
under the microscope for them, it too becomes textured, a ridged,

vallied, mountained terrain like Saturn under the clouds that
are hazy lab coats. The world powers race to put the first man
there, crave another success like Cain's. Doctors give their
daughters healing. My father gave me the way to patch rubber, the
way to resume the ride on air that flat tires interrupt. Lungs

failed him. The doctors, their daughters saw it coming, knew
what it was, left the room so they could be alone, but I
would not; I stayed and they did it anyway, in front of me.
Sleazy, indecent the way death got intimate with him while
I watched, inadvertent voyeur perhaps but damned good at it,

expert after one session—yet not envied at all.
The progression of the pictures shows my mother filling
like a hot air balloon, hoarding the air her husband would
have used, holding his breaths so tenderly, so sweetly that
of course she looks pregnant, of course she has this evidence
of making love. Of course she resists laboring and envying
those who need work at nothing.

TORNADOS

Truth is, I envy them
not because they dance; I out jitterbug them
as I'm shuttled through and through legs
strong as looms, weaving time. They
do black more justice than I, frenzy
of conductor of philharmonic and electricity, hair
on end, result of the charge when horns and strings release
the pent up Beethoven and Mozart. Ions played

instead of notes. The movement
is not wrath, not hormone swarm because
I saw my first forming above the church a surrogate
steeple. The morning of my first baptism and
salvation already tangible, funnel for the spirit
coming into me without losing a drop, my black
guardian angel come to rescue me before all the words

get out, *I looked over Jordan and what did I see coming for*
to carry me home. Regardez, it all comes back, even the first
grade French, when the tornado stirs up the past, bewitched spoon
lost in its own spin, like a roulette wheel that won't
be steered, like the world. They drove me underground,
tornado watches and warnings, atomic bomb drills. Adult
storms so I had to leave the room. Truth is

the tornado is a perfect nappy curl, tightly wound,
spinning wildly when I try to tamper with its nature, shunning
the hot comb and pressing oil even though if absolutely straight
I'd have the longest hair in the world. Bouffant tornadic
crown taking the royal path on a trip to town, stroll down
Tornado Alley where it intersects Memory Lane. Smoky spirit-
clouds, shadows searching for what cast them.

HIGHWAY 29: A PEDESTRIAN'S VIEW

It's a long walk to Culpepper. By
the end of it, Blue Ridge shadows
are smoked teeth and the earth
is about to be swallowed. Not that

Culpepper is bad conscience; there in
a house whose white is faltering is a
tiny orange (when the sun is right, but
when is it wrong?) woman whose long
fingers and broad, blunt nails pull

life into the world, make sure it's
gone before the last tucking in. Few
but she will kiss the hardened cheeks
of strangers. And there's a hardware

store's smorgasbord of #6 common nails thick
as shoestring licorice, screws like striped
peppermints sucked gray; sold by the pound,
cheaper than sirloin. I check road signs

for specials, willing to buy 20 rolls
of good thick paper towels fit for
sanitary napkins on a day I must pioneer
to live it, if the bargain is true, based

on need not quota; limit, two per customer.
Geometry. Signs cut like faceted gems and
license plates like the rare rectangular blue
diamond; gemologists and convicts' cusping.

Jewels pronounce the roadway's conniptions: dips,
oblique rude turns, skid marks like flat obelisks
at the sudden change in direction, cold shoulder
even desired later, up ahead where the sign, a

good gypsy, says none. The veering spouse,
blonde glint dominating his (this time) eye,
blind spot where the wife would be, cruising
a humped road, riding on breasts, buttocks

juggled sideways, hula if hands were talking, a
fast girl, hot ticket since they're not. Miss It
walking and stopping traffic. *Hey, Baby, you sweet*
Georgia brown thing. I ain't no diabetic yet and
you a long way from home. She is unimpressed; this

is Culpepper and rust is metallic sunset. Ordinary.
Exactly as it should be, nods the orange midwife
listening to the scant echo of a heartbeat, the
ticking at the ceiling of the womb, passage of all
the generations of time, through the tunnel, across
the bridge, stem, blithe weeping at the crossroads,
the head blossoming between soft thighs. This is return.

THE PLACE THAT MAKES PRESIDENTS

I am there not understanding what

it is about these white churches set God's stride
apart, wooden guilt of fences charting the range
of a prayer. Every moment is one of those
quiet ones stolen from Roxbury or Mattapan left with
noisy violence, loud poverty that sound like gibberish
when the language is solitude as it is here, but such
an old theft, it has the respect of age, the
benefit of history, tradition of the acquisition
of the continent. Quietly a crime becomes heroic. Like

a secret southern ballot, old-fashioned, the good-old-days,
not-so-good nights of hit-lynch-and-run. Trains
speed by, electric rivers (down which runaways were resold)
whistling belligerent self-righteous sermons to which I
yield right of way; then comes reward, the lifting of the
railroad crossing gate like a sword finishing the
bestowal of knighthood. How fitting

a commemoration for the Goody Saras, "Young Goodman Browns"
and the rest, the Tituba too much a lighthouse, too much
the defiling beacon with aimed light that lifts veils
too many nights before the wedding, peeping through closed
curtains of fog behind which virginity is peeled off, draped
across the chair, put back on with the petticoat and pants in
time for the ceremony. Living here is ceremonial. Elitist

operating procedure. Pilgrim privilege. Yankee superiority, no
slavery here, just the Blue Vein Society for the fair, the just
skinned; coon shows with *African Delineators* with bootblacked
faces a fist could shine—I don't mock the place; I

love it, marvel at its talents, witches and presidents
made here, horses shoed here, fresh eggs laid here, Smolak's

apples, Putnam's cider press, Whittle and Belson's cranberries,
Martha's Vineyard, Woonsocket to incant like Gidget calling
her Moondoogie, hungrier than a wolf, the syllables glistening
in her mouth like moons that guide he-wolf to she-wolf, pelt
estrous-slick; Winnepesaukee as the next day's love, sixteen
and adaptable (not fickle; these are changing times),
young colonies learning rights—too numerous to list—the bill
of rights so named to make known the cost, the prejudices paid
in full for exploring from your own first-time point of view only,

assuming something better will be found based on the track record:
discovery of the continent itself, tall ships whose arrival
conquered canoes; and it did come, a rush of gold like a blast
of opium and it was slavery all over again. . . . Return to

quieter time, gentler nation; Wild West, Bill Hickok, Earp
and Jesse James but rumors. Billy the Kid as our American Peter
Pan. Gun runners = Olympic contenders. Continue to focus
on how the West was won. Ignore loss. Maintain the American
Dream, American morale, Marilyn Monroe's face on Miss Liberty,
she won't discriminate, the tired, hungry, poor, huddled masses;
Marilyn also lures the rich, the political, the unscrupulous, the
not fully weaned. Trust Wonsfellow's cheese while you wait

for autumn to come, red as a dream of leeches once required
of doctors, not even close to vision-quest. The panacea
capital still with Harvard's medical and business schools. Yale's
a second opinion away. And still possible to go to Salem for
a haunting, though not necessary to go so far. No matter where,
someone preceded me; I am nudged along by reclaiming spirits who
need the understanding I need so that we can sleep on beds for
which geese, Narragansett and Passamaquoddy were plucked.

DETOUR: THE DEATH OF AGNES

The night that smelled of cigarettes,
dirty snow like piles of matted ashes.

Over my shoulder in Danbury, Connecticut
my father's thin hands wiped the rear window
and I could see more clearly behind me than
in front, the road curling back there like
possibility, future, not dead past where I

recall my father rushing readiness, me nine
months old in some kind of ersatz hiking boots
retooled from his belts; he had no intention of
ever spanking me. That Sunday, I kicked up dust

that he said was me, the flying I'd do till
I could soar. I picked up a rock that he said
was me, under my pillow that night keeping me
awake, aware, more-or-less spherical bulwark,
practically immortal, my igneous self in my hand
tasting faintly sweet, fluctuating salty. He

claimed he drove a Mercury before I was born, knew
when to stop. He once had a Studebaker dream but
couldn't smell the bakery in that so we walked
from then on, full off the smell; that was the wonder
of Wonder Bread—we didn't have to buy any; almost
got rich. Any rocks in the way were cousins come

for reunion. Cancer's not the only way to go but
is effective. Agnes' lungs were not lungs, pneumatic
flops, an old woman's flat breasts ingrown. Gestures.
Her liver was there in name only, picture of catharsis.
The year of our Lord 1980 and Calvin leaves. 1990 and
his sister Agnes. The zero years. The nothing years.
My father riding again in a Toyota, a Corolla Deluxe but
he died anyway. I hadn't meant ten years ago to

drive a hearse, my hands on the horn blessing the
blaring Isaac while the back seat patriarch, his eyes
glowing like the sky leopard's spots, went hungry
for such touching. Forgiveness

jumps in this blessed/cursed night, the hitchhiker
I didn't stop for, determined to ride. I can steer
the car to locations besides death, I learned or my
father would not taxi again with me, would have
learned from his mistake of having me save him, of
having me at all, of marrying my mother, who
ended up alone anyway, just as if he hadn't.

Isn't *Agnes* a biblical book quoted almost as often
as *Psalms?* Doctors opened her and saw no scriptures,
no prophecy, no words or mark of God; ravaged and
mangled organs: Nazi science that we couldn't go by
to identify the body. Instead, by what we felt near
it, just coming into the room, her hair short like
curtains tied way back to let in all the light that
can come in her Halsted Avenue home.

It is of course the right road, the asphalt just
the black backing of a girdling, constricting mirror
that also is a vehicle to the world of Tennessee
geese, chickens in morning feathers like the
continuation of Brasier dreams knocked only once
out of the ballpark by the same ball that
struck their brother Homer Edgar dead.

The geese honk and honk for their riders and
drivers. My grandmother before Homer's funeral
throws down grain, exact toll change, and the
chickens gather around the luck that an hour earlier
rain would have washed away

as sure as Ethel Waters knew *Darkies never dream.*
Thin hands one night pull down the moon and stars
making you detour into a field of luminous cotton
that you would call Heaven if you could.

DENNIS'S SKY LEOPARD

He saw it first, me just the big, the
little dippers and questions about
when they'd be full, ready to pour
something into me, anything, not just
what I've needed so long I've forgotten
what it is. He said

"I love him." How familiar
that sounded; I love him too, the one
steering the planets, a very male
thing to do; a woman admits to difficulty
in just navigating one small life, maneuvering
it away from diapers, last minute trips to Messina's
for bell peppers that don't chime, for both
angel and devil's food cake mixes to hide the truth,
for sugarless gum, sugarless colas and lemon limes,
ginger drinks full of pin pricks,

because the honeymoon is over; the grace period
is gone; the music must be faced now, rock lyrics
that slap with the full force of Rolling Stones,
verifying that you're the only sinner in the world.
Dennis said, "He's up in the air." I tried
to suck him up my nose. Dennis said, "He can't
come down." So he defies gravity, he breaks
bad laws, he's a male Antigone, a man I'd like
to meet if he weren't a leopard
and without domestic instincts like men.

This leopard takes up the whole sky, decorated
(as in purple, love-bruised hearts)
with constellations, star-quality spots.
He lives better up there than in the jungle.
Rain is attempt at spot give-away. They melt.
Something about our atmosphere and hospitality.

I tilt my head, let it rain in my throat. Inside
I feel like a wheat field ready for perfect
harvest leading to ultimate feast but I'm never
cut down. That's the best part.

WHAT HUNG ABOVE OUR HEADS LIKE TRUCE

was also sky we think we cannot touch but
with eyes; horizons stay put like sadnesses.

What we would not even pray for
in the alcove our hands make, was

already true: *even the one-eyed mother selling mangoes
in the street makes sure her child looks great,*

the white flounce collar peeled away from her throat
like the white fish flesh filleted by cool hands whose
long fingers forecast nimbus.

Cooked, the fillets seemed feathered as the dream
of a manta ray whose wings stir Atlantic salt
that dissolves as if sweet in the presence of Humpbacks
and Narwahls spraying fireworks, dolphins at the end of dives
pinning foam corsages on the waves.

There is some restitution after all.

This time when I hear them, I answer the church bells and
hear voices across the skinny phone wires and the fat snakes:

*Did you call the synagogue?
Aren't you Rosenthal the butcher?*

You don't realize that you don't know answers until
you hear questions.

Besides, would the collar and flounder be enough
to disprove butchery? Instead
the wrong number hears a sound too tiny for the cocking
of a gun, too sympathetic for a clock, but something
clicks, falls into place.

Be advised that we talked Xhosa, made love
as the one-eyed woman, all her mangoes in other hands,
finished a tea biscuit, stardust
falling from her lips onto flounder scales, aware
of the heaviness of all that light and that heaven
pressing, pressing down.

ALMOST AN ODE TO THE WEST INDIAN MANATEE

Once James Balog had said *her snout was soft as deerskin*
but the rest of her hide had the rough tautness of a football
made of sandpaper that was ode enough.

In the facing photo, the hamadryas baboon snubs me, her
nose's uptilt such that the nostrils are mosques
dark with shed sins and the doom that opposes pilgrimage.
She is in love.

I'll buy that; what can't happen at a Florida circus
with twin monkey girls (their hair like pipeworks follows
the spines beneath their costumes exiting mid-rump slits like
prehensile tails neglected into dredlock rip off) and a resident
hawker whose chest hair grows in question marks. Also

Guernsey cow with six stomachs each separately fed by the
angle of head at grazing, the particulars of the lowing, variety
of the moo, the sweetness of the quackgrass and clover
and all the different mood-matched milks on country tables
in pitchers with pouring lips wide as a pelvic bone.

The rhino's horn hollowed out is cornucopian. I never
think of this when it would do some good. Already
the manatee and baboon are starting to taste extinction,
welcoming it as resolution of a forgotten craving deep in
the proliferation of Guernsey cream white as a light-emitting
lake that makes manatee and baboon glow when they catch sight
of themselves during their dive at the moment in which
the dive becomes inevitable, the cream displacing
into a crown as they enter, then settling
as if they never existed.

THE NATURE OF MORNING

With arm at the angle for low salute
each tooth is brushed, up and down, anticipating
the next duty of raising the flag, full vs half
staff, I can never decide; only officially is
there sometimes reason not to mourn. Forks
of sunlight come down as from a farmer stuffing
clouds into his blue silo trying not to sink in
it, trying not to go under, but it's so clear, so
uncomplicated, easier to make sense of than
foreclosure in which he'll drown anyway. A rake of rays
untangles grasses, separates as

in hugs having to end, trains having to pull away,
these things whose attraction is in sameness, coalition
contrary to the governing magnetism. *Amandla.*
It helps to smile, to reveal as many teeth as
possible for better brushing, reduced decay.
They should sparkle and gleam, not yellow into
brittle pages, obsolesence of the saved first soft-
sided shoe, saved pacifier never in peril. The
yellowed wedding dress, its shoulders padded, skirt
petticoated so that an actual bride is unnecessary
just as she was the wedding day.

Here's a reason to mourn: letting the best man get
away, marrying a lesser, non-superlative groom. It
happens at every wedding. Mistakes
are any nation's chief product. Apology
travels incognito, in the form of toothbrush, in
the form of maid, doing my dirty work for me, keeping
my hands clean, business as usual, elbows off the
table, grace before the meal in which teeth
could be innocent bystanders were they not gladiators.
All that I don't doubt is the nature of a thing.

POEM FOR MY MOTHERS AND OTHER MAKERS OF ASAFETIDA

Brown in the bottle, my
honeyed memory of my grandmother in
which I drench myself, pour over myself
one of her tight hugs, homemade gravy on
lips and ribs, eventually hips, *taste her, taste her*
and feast on my church in a bottle, the
gospel like Sis. Posey sings it, *oh when, when will
I get home?* Looking over Dixie, over
Jordan, river of life, needing to cross (already got
a cross), needing to swim to *Jordan's stormy
other shore,* listen: the brown choir's brown liquid voice,
my arms moving me through it, swimming is just directing
the choir, giving instructions, *Mama always told me to be still
sometimes and feel the power,* wait while the river moves down my
throat, urine the rest of the miracle that makes of me
a fountain; nasty asafetida, tastes like the bootleg, jackleg
medicine it is
curing me as only generations can, asafetida is *a quilt
for my innards,* she said, up to her neck in gizzards, hocks, pickled
pig's feet, her hands good as dull knives that can't
have accidents.
And everywhere, everywhere eggs like teeth big as
what memory does to Grandma. Even the heart of gold.

Finally
the asafetida toast just after gunfire, the new year
shot for coming uninvited, ahead of schedule, years
coming and going, out of control, Trojan years bringing
lots of what we don't want set loose in foreclosed fields
of stone potatoes so hardhearted, hardheaded there are
no eyes except the ones I look into and fall in love, right
into Mama's pupils, the past dark with dense ancestry, all
who came before having to fit into the available space of
history which is existence's memory and year after year
the overcrowding worsens, *remember, remember: darkest before*

the day every dog will have, we are dogs sometimes, vestiges
of our evolution giving us dreams, instincts, secrets for dark
recall; nothing really goes away
especially not that sickening paradox, falling to reach
the sublime emotion; want to rise in love, want a boost,
elevator ride to the penthouse, silk jacket smoking
with lust, man making it with an asafetida bottle, a glass
mama with an excuse for breaking; whatever sustains you is your
mama, that wall holding back wind, jazz on the airwaves and in
the Thunderbird, the Boone's Farm; the oar smacking discipline
into fish while ferrying you across the water
that takes you back to old Virginny, every visit is return
to the scene of crimes, so much happened there, so much history
there; rivers are sad affairs flowing between past and future
like pompous blue (if sunny) ribbons that must deepen, widen
or spill to really go anywhere and still there are limits,
disillusionment to cap any growth, live to the fullest and just
have more to lose to death but Grandma said, Mama says, now
I say: *maybe possible to have so much*
death can't take it all; asafetida still on the shelf, oil in the puddle
still ghetto stained glass, still rainbow remnants in rock
bottom ghetto sky like a promise of no more tears, asafetida
bottle floating there, some kind of Moses, some kind of deliverer,
there's always a way. Away means not here. Place where bagpipes echo
with sound of a stuck doll calling *Mama, Mama,* nothing but
    inspiration
in the air, and the prophet Jolson proclaiming *Mammy,* asking for
her who can make him wash his face; she's the one who can turn it
    into
something to love.

II

BIRMINGHAM BROWN'S TURN

I know how ridiculous this could seem, the
moon as one of Birmingham Brown's pop eyes when
he's admiring Charlie Chan as living

icon, but I can't stop seeing the magic, even
as Birmingham drives Charlie around
in a car black as Birmingham, black as

compliment, emulation, and adoration. Ridiculous
were it not wonderful, Birmingham's enormous
feel for the night, moving in it

like something made for it, made
of it; the city, every city wearing
his face at night, his smile a

handy lantern—ooh; marvel at those skyscrapers
that pushed up from underground like
flowers; their office lights

come on like petals opening, the
cleaning ladies there like bees
busy pollinating, pulling buckets

of nectar with umbilical arms, honeying
the floors till the sweet glow
pops out, a girlish event, a knowing

and liking puberty's entitlement.
How can anyone who thinks the place
is one big apple understand? It's

a whole damned apple orchard! I
realize that Birmingham is supposed
to be insult, a debit not credit

to his race; we're just ashamed
that his costume and mask fit so
well, as if we believe that clothes

make men, but hear this and hear this
well: no polyester, no rayon or
charmeuse blouse is my creator. And

consider; his performance—according
to script, not autobiography by the way—
did not lower the bottom-hugging black

race. And anyway, what if
the world—knowing how crazy it is
documented to be—is traveling upside

down; what if Birmingham is on the
top? The night sure treats him
royally; he glides through it as though

in a coach; it sure pampers him, opens
itself so that walking towards you
he disappears before reaching you; the

night, a woman dark, passionate, heavy with
her love, pulls him into her secret
chambers, won't give anyone a chance at

taste. I don't know names, never had to
consider nationality, just race; black is black
everywhere in the world. Dark moments,

pestilences tend to dominate our minds, stand
out like sentries though what they guard
is unclear. Despite this, *Ustinov* to me

sounds more Russian than *Georgia* that to me
is a conjure word summoning the cotillion
and pecan eyes, pies, and earlobes; peaches

rushing to shave off what's just now
telling the world they're men. But authentic
Atlanta (accept no imitation) men have

a way of saying what they are that won't
let the world forget. I don't mind
the beard stuck on Ustinov, it seems made

of the appropriate rice for effigy,
caricature. And that broken English
tripping out his mouth appropriately

in bound footsteps. Now how would it look
for Charlie Chan not to be recognizably
Chinese especially when Ustinov cannot

draw from his rickshaw infancy, his
ideographic preschool scribbles, his
chopstick crutches to help him eat

moo goo gai pan, his first words, before
even *mamasan* or *papasan* or is that
Japanese? Who can tell just

by looking at his face, the Russian
stubble poking through to ferret out
Viet Cong, Viet anything, Hmong women

just as good, even Cambodian though
they can lean too Polynesian looking so
back off, spare them. As for the rest,

see one, you've seen them all, hovering
above the number one son like a mist
to cool his face, so hot

under the make-up that upsets, tilts
his eyes. Appropriately. Asian eyes
being the claim to fame. And silk.

You can bet that Charlie can take you
to the cleaners; isn't he Chinese?
Don't they boil the clothes and the

rice in the same woks? Isn't this
the year of the horse, the broken,
tamed stallion? Of the Mongoloid

Idiot? Of Peking sitting duck? That's
what Charlie said, I think, talking
in his sleep, parallel to his geisha,

together the models for the railroad
tracks, just straighten the cross's
horizontal arm, lengthen both to infinity,
crucify the same....

Ride the *chop chop* trains instead of *choo choos;*
they're just as rhythmic, hypnotic, still
punctuated with joy as the train moves in and

out of shadows cast when a Hiroshima girl's
thousand cranes fly by the sun; their
silhouettes are exclamation marks.

I still dream of it, digging to China,
going through the center of the earth's
meaning to earn passage there. I want

that moment that worms complete
their evolution into egg rolls and my
dandruff is recycled into bait that

entices some junk boat occupants
to take me in because they're the ones
who walk on water all the time.

To hell with Peter, that's what my
fortune cookie said; either one,
Ustinov or Jesus' right hand man.

Going there, having passed through
the hellish center to get there, I notice
how Jesus becomes Confucius without a hitch
and can keep his parables, his disciples

if he wishes; I can keep salvation,
so can Birmingham. Who cares
what he *may* have lost.

TIME FOR PRAISE

for Dennis and Craig

Finally that season too has come, a reason
to put anger and evil somewhere other than
on the front lines. The mercenary in us can
for the moment be lulled or drugged—do what's

necessary—to sleep. There's an eclipse going
on, the usual ultra-violet is being blocked by
a dark force that is not evil, at least not
while being Samaritan. Not quite magic per se
just a time for other, weaker realities to

emerge, those that have been camouflaged. Tonight
I say only because it is dark and no name yet
exists for dark daytime. Language is known for
accuracy less than for lies. Tonight brook trout
won't bite. Perch will swim on as if no fine

line between things that aren't different anyway is
in the water. The fresh water. Meaning too-forward
water, precocious water clamoring to get inside us
as a way past our superficiality. The salt seasoned
water, great bodies of it, all the salt, the meaning

of the earth simplified into liquid and we can't drink
until we're enough like God to tolerate ambrosia. Take
heart; tonight might be the night our status changes.
Follow the leader, the boy casting his line in traffic

and reeling in a Toyota, a whale with a door that the
Jonah inside with his wife and just-born couldn't see.
They were en route to a hospital, they were aware that
birth is an emergency, that we are under siege whenever

something comes into the world and can't leave the way
it came. It must forge like Lewis and Clark, raise past
taxes like Dukakis; it must leave salt-sea origin and
walk on land then die to become useful minerals and

elements. Tonight though, a centerfold reads like the
periodic table, the atomic numbers are her measurements.
And that Toyota, whale on wheels, tonight it's a chariot;
tomorrow, stinking, rotting meat once a little light is

shed, as from a sun going bald or with dandruff; either way
something's wrong with it. We won't know of the sun's
hijacking till eight minutes after it happens. And then
it won't matter; that lingering, false light will be

airtight alibi telling us
there's been no crime.

THE JONAH EFFECT

Instead of mud, frisbees (plastic hubcaps) on
the ground, the fifties car was there, long
as a hearse, white as memory, Pythagorean fins

warning of sharkiness in the medium navigated,
reckless drivers changing lanes along the hypotenuse
of three-way affairs so that a majority

may rule. This was not, however, a day to retreat
into Marilyn Monroe doctrine of sarong with busty
sharkiness cutting, into the medium being navigated,

an image of woman she could not reach herself.
I was through with all that; I looked out the
window that day to see ahead, androgynous picket

fences surrounding me instead of boned corsets
and their Jonah effect. In Nineveh, as in Sodom,
the doctrine of harlots, the chorus of strumpets,

the gospel of self-seduction. The car was sent
for me, the vacant back seat where statutory rape
registers, the triangle of legs as if only geometry

is at hand. The car's nuptial paint job lies about
the condition of the bride, a bomb has been dropped
on her, as a mother she is ruined, as a nationality

she is ruined; when she looks out the window
she won't be able to find Saigon, her children
won't answer to their names but she won't be

able to call them *Rumplestiltskin,* the cure
for an archaic disease; something else
ails us, *Aids* that sounds like cure, *emphysema*

that sounds like an Indian word for a beautiful land
form, like the fifty-first state or its capital.
An automatic transmission, just sit back; cruise

control, just ride, just be a tourist in the past
because you can't change a damn thing, just live
it over and over again. White car, white whale,

white dress,
all white as a sheet,
all scared.

SPECIAL EFFECTS

I am overwhelmed by the unprecedented
accuracy of fear.

Consider how I almost scalded it in coffee, the
spoon I mistook as a key piece of my knight's armor
sure to bring him back. How could a spoon's
full, sterling hip diminishing into leg longer,
smoother than the signature Grable gam fail?
As backup: a flock of hangers perched on the
closet rod beside the heel of my shoe and when
these meet, there is that high note of a crystal
triangle to finish what the soprano can but start;
that same metaphysical note, just an octave lower
still higher than Fay Wray's screams.
She was a spoon in Kong's hand.

Tonight's feature is *Kronos,* a
technological monster, walking mega-mousetrap,
berserk Erector set of a puberty-plagued demon.
His legs were refinery storage tanks and I
will forever understand pistons from the way
he walked (kind of a mobile trash compactor).
Grendel in armor. Knight of the electromagnetic
table. Quest of the Holy Wattage. And vegetarian,
eater strictly of power plants.

He could be made of millions of spoons
melted down and reforged.
Live by the silver spoon, die by the silver spoon
when Kronos squashes you.

When Santa was younger, thinner with dark hair
and unemployed he was probably Maynard G. Krebs,
artificial beatnik. What a scary thought.

Everything a spoon has going for it
sooner or later slides off

For instance, I am not afraid of flying but of
failing to fly.

INTERPRETATION OF A POEM BY FROST

A young black girl stopped by the woods,
so young she knew only one man: Jim Crow
but she wasn't allowed to call him Mister.
The woods were his and she respected his boundaries
even in the absence of fence.
Of course she delighted in the filling up
of his woods, she so accustomed to emptiness,
to being taken at face value.
This face, her face eternally the brown
of declining autumn, watches snow inter the grass,
cling to bark making it seem indecisive
about race preference, a fast-to-melt idealism.
With the grass covered, black and white are the only options,
polarity is the only reality; corners aren't neutral
but are on edge.
She shakes off snow, defiance wasted
on the limited audience of horse.
The snow does not hypnotize her as it wants to,
as the blond sun does in making too many prefer daylight.
She has promises to keep,
the promise that she bear Jim no bastards,
the promise that she ride the horse only as long
as it is willing to accept riders,
the promise that she bear Jim no bastards,
the promise to her face that it not be mistaken as shadow,
and miles to go, more than the distance from Africa to Andover
more than the distance from black to white
before she sleeps with Jim.

THE LYNCHING

They should have slept, would have
but had to fight the darkness, had
to build a fire and bathe a man in
flames. No

other soap's as good when
the dirt is the skin. Black since
birth, burnt by birth. His father
is not in heaven. No parent

of atrocity is in heaven. My father chokes
in the next room. It is night, darkness
has replaced air. We are white like
incandescence

yet lack light. The God in my father
does not glow. The only lamp
is the burning black man. Holy
burning, holy longing, remnants of

a genie after greed. My father
baptizes by fire same as
Jesus will. Becomes a holy ghost when
he dons his sheet, a clerical collar

out of control, Dundee Mills percale,
fifty percent cotton, dixie, confederate
and fifty percent polyester, man-made, man-
ipulated, unnatural, mulatto fiber, warp

of miscegenation.
After the bath, the man is hung as if
just his washed shirt, the parts
of him most capable of sin removed.

Charred, his flesh is bark, his body
a trunk. No sign of roots. I can't leave
him. This is limbo. This is the life after
death coming if God is an invention as were

slaves. So I spend the night, his thin moon-begot
shadow as mattress; something smouldering
keeps me warm. Patches of skin fall onto me
in places I didn't know needed mending.

PREFERABLE TRUTH

I'm glad I ate the cigarette; it's
good to celebrate lessons, a lie
of course but I'm a mother
inventing preferable truth.

All one-year-olds want feeding
and I did it for myself, gleaming
wonderling, already two months (my mother's
lie) out of diapers. Toddling sophisticate
with superb hand-eye coordination

and an hors d'oeuvre in an ashtray. Pity
that long, slim white things weren't meant
to sustain me, long Caucasion history served
in a smorgasbord of texts. How well

I remember Columbus' discovery: America
could be bought if he sold it to himself. I
lack the stomach for the work, the Constitution
mine but recently. 1956 and Rosa Parks
already comfortable is when doctors

pumped my stomach, nurses landing in Mt. Sinai's
halls on milk legs, on long white dreaminess.
The curtain pulled round me was snowy wing of
something that could lift itself and me. How

did I know so soon to want lifting? I'd see
nothing but my mother put on white stockings and
raise her half-scissors leg, aim her toes
to rip the center out of a nylon
doughnut. Then she'd knot the stockings in

cancerous lumps just below her knees, all power
even her own, working against her. Long, slim
conspiracy. And oh yes; my Easter chicken died
when our attic home was painted white to enlarge
it, give it power of deceit, the right to

conspire; no ventilation, chick had no
breathing room, my ancestors likewise embalmed
in the grade and secondary school pages, mummies,
gifts no one rips apart to possess. *What's*

wrong with us? Wasn't it enough,
our lemming leaps into the Atlantic, diving
into baptism that couldn't wait, drinking
the holy water too for deep, deep cleansing when
we jumped slave ship? The world

had never seen such repentance! Our
lungs full of it, breathing water holier than
air always touching me, touching me, making
advances I'd prefer that air, the invisible empire
of the south (and north), not make.

THE LINOLEUM RHUMBA

On parade: some of the dancer's many personalities and
guises, the Nelson's cook, the Peabody's domestic,
the geriatric ward's bed pan handler and

her children: child of the babushka, child of
the do-rag, child of the scarf, child of the veil,
child of the wig, child of the tortilla, child of
pita, child of hominy, cornpone, and grits.

Some think she's going to shine the podium and
it's true that her bosom dusts it as she speaks:
I left Mississippi for Toledo.
I left Toledo for Watts.
Thought I would see light, but
we can't stay here, we can't live this way
all by instinct but not the instinct
bred in Toogaloo and fed Pearl water.
What my children need are commando strategies that
you'd think being who and what I am I would have.
My sour lemons are the most like grenades but
they make our mouths pucker and all we can talk about
then is brotherly love.
I've also got diamonds and spades, hearts and clubs
that I keep passing out to my young ones but Lord
if my eldest doesn't keep throwing his on the table.
I don't want him shot, so I let him shoot nothing,
not the breeze, not a family picture, not hoops.

Let me clear up a nagging misunderstanding: this
is the way to make the white woman's bed—she thinks
I make it because she is rich, she thinks I make it
to get her money, that I can't get money any other
way, no skills, no intelligence, no contribution to
society but for her four poster, but I make her bed
because on Judgment Day, you will have to sleep

in the bed you made and I make damn good ones but
she didn't make any.

Enter the cat pawing its way out of the bag and into
the cat house on Catfish Row, no story completely believed
without nasty black women, their shortchanged alphabet,
from D to W, domestic to whore, sheets binding them, their
fishnet stockings hooking innocent men trying to be disciples
or they wouldn't be studying no net.

Know what she does? Goes right on loving that man limb
by limb, the mop right out of a stick figure drawing
and something to smile about: *only the flesh is weak and*
ain't none of that on him nowhere. They're
going out tonight, a heavy date, even dancing.

Sunday found her on the mourner's bench. The song
closed in on her: *Oh, loose that man and let him go.*
Then she knew; her mop is the rib, staff of Moses, spigot
for the rock water coming then, from her clay heart, her
Mississippi mud face, tributary with Niagara destiny cutting
to the bone, leaping from chin to breast, and THUNDER so
her Lord can call her and she can answer like lightning, a
bold blaze, slap across Master's fresh face, ruddy as
the cut flowers brought in this morning to grace the altar
she'd swept clean of petals, flower crap, rose and
carnation doo doo, perfume not so much mask as sweet synonym.
She had what she needed.

She returns to the podium, kicks the cat off
the platform, speaks: *Children, ain't a damn thing to*
be sorry for this morning.

The huge crowd doesn't know what to do as
they've come resolved to apologize.

GREEN LIGHT AND GAMMA WAYS

My brother, two years in the world and
exhausted, sits, porcelain bowl on his head,
for a haircut. An all-purpose bowl, we
aren't too good to beg with it. We do
because we are good, deserving. Uncooked
rice and quarters sound the same filling it.

I am immobilized, in a red light
district. The triple XXX's on the marquis
are my parents' legal signature
and approval, my embarrassment. I hope
I don't turn red, Communist. Lichis and
tadpoles holler, the crickets tick, New
World luck, westward

expansion thanks to dynamite, Grandfather's
fingers some of the Santa Fe and Southern
Pacific lines's spikes. Crucified
by my color, sick of it, jaundiced, yellow fever,
tropical, oriental.

No one speaks this old railroad language,
the locomotive blues, no speed, no
action till a rage of steam riots. Black
fist engine through a tunnel to African
rebirth. Reroutings to the Shabazz Station
roundhouse for instructions, identity. Role
models. My nose and mouth as full as theirs,
as much potential. *Say it loud, I'm Black and
I'm proud* and there is thunder. *Say it loud,
I'm yellow and proud* and there is cheese
to stand alone, *hi-ho, the derri-o, the cheese
stands alone.*

My aunt Mei-Ting, too old for everything, has
mummy feet. Better known as lotuses, flowers,
vehicles for guilt trip, gifts for the binding
anniversary. She walks in vases. She won't

go far. Beware the trip to podiatrists.
Beware of legal fetish. Gamma ways.

My mother tells how the boat brought her
to the arms of Miss Liberty, her new mother.
She bowed long, low. Demanded nothing, didn't claim
her rights. *I have nothing to declare.* My mother
serves, the homage of rice cakes, fish, tofu and
potatoes left on the porch for helpful,
avenging spirits. *Cats. Rats.* I say.

Miss Liberty is green, the horizon and sky
plus my yellow skin. She is a minority too.
Color of ridiculous Martian fable. And not a man.
Handicapped, disabled. Green Moslem veil.

Another immigrant. I was born
American; I know cover-up is not the answer.
Peel and strip, bump and grind, Boston's Chinatown
in the Combat Zone, as if the boys and
their war brought home. Twenty-five

cents can still buy a book, a love
manual, a first generation girl's
allowance, as long as it's English
she can learn from it, first in
her low class, *e-c-h-e-l-o-n,*
echelon and she wins the spelling bee

while the sting operation works toward
light change, against red monopoly.
Green light is like the Pacific.
Green light is like jade.
Money changes, transforms hands, Green light
is like the power you envy. It is shined on
Miss Liberty, has no inner genesis. But it
warms her.

MISS LIBERTY LOSES PAGEANT

Should be a headline but it's not
newsworthy, more ordinary than anchovies
gossipping olfactions of fishy scandal.

The Lady of the Harbor, Fatima rip-off
except she came first with a crown like
the one of thorns on another whose cause is

masses. Avant-garde refugee from 50's horror
flick *Attack of the 50-foot Woman,* here turned
to stone fleeing Gomorrah, Gotham, some G (god-

damned) place. *There she is, Miss America, your
ideal;* there must be a mistake, Miss Liberty
should have won. Why was there a contest? And

what about that talent? Professional model, posed,
picture perfect. Mannequin displayed where the world
window shops. In case of emergency, break glass.

She lost her fire. Holds an ice-cream cone.
Maybe she'll court Prometheus, this green old
paradoxical maid in Spinster Army uniform.

Basic Training long over, revolutions too
yet she earned no stars or stripes, no rank,
not even private; she's public, communal,

free. How happy she must be, everyday
at the beach, keeping to the shallows, barely
up to her knees. No lifeguard is on duty.

Her back is to us while she changes
her mind about walking away, entering
the deep seat of meaning she thought furnished

her house. She sits at the water table,
a feast has been laid for Squanto or Hobbamock
and she is it. They will be converts. Guests

not hosts. A hot night in July, fireworks
popping instead of corn. These are new ways
of business as usual. The struggle to be taken

seriously prevails over the better instinct of
not being taken at all. She is in moonlight,
her toes loosen caviar, if the sun gets the angle

right, it will sink in her torch and proxy a candle.
How romantic is the notion. Better that she gets
the man than Dudley Do-Right whose name is plea.

LONGING TO SEE A NURTURING GRAVE

for Sharifa Al-Homaizi

Something about a graveyard makes me confident,
the tombstones behind my back like accurate
histories; only the dead are fully equipped.
Something about it makes me weave and want to be
cloth, my legs lockstitched into the earth so that
I may be fed directly, from bottom up, not top down,
reversing discrimination. Who cares who died.

With fifty other women I obliged gender that
day. All dressed up and no funeral to go to.
"Stay home, don't trouble yourself," he said
aware of female abilities. We of the kitchen
serve milk, blood, tears: recipe for life. We are
counted on, counted out, figured out; mathematics:
the male weapon beyond our aptitude. The menstrual
cycle numbers our days for us. At the end, the
grave takes us in, doesn't chew us up, spit us out or
threaten paternal brimstone. Mother's love triumphs.

Besides, I need to know how it's done, this
entering the ground Houdini style in
vaults of steel, embalmed into virtual steel
yourself; I need to know just how miraculous
getting up from that will be even
if afterwards I just go to hell.

NEWS

for Randy and Laura

Don't say again that no news is good
news, don't judge another event; right
and wrong is not the agenda of the history
we live; the purpose is to pass time, while
away the hours, appear to be moving.

Don't hate me because I'm beautiful and saying
it, narcissism can keep you going when nothing
else will. Builds your character, possible
to acquire a gargantuan structure and if you
do, then what a fortress! Ghosts

are in the woods and rightly so, daybreak
rays come in guise of apparitional negligee
that my soul can wear and still be beautiful
without a body. A haunting is but a thought

coming from other than your narcissism so
it's suspect. A haunting is the evicted
demanding multi-cultural equity. You bet
that can scare the pants off somebody but

hopefully more than just the pants. Some
prejudices coming off too would be nice.
Then stark nakedness, the body as wasted
land, exploited land, deforested, Eden

without trees, knowledge impossible, sex
as unfruitful attempt at grafting; go ahead,
try to run away from all that, steal a
Volvo, sleep in it in the surviving woods
and think you've got it

made; sorcery has nothing up on you because
even without it, what created sorcery still
is in the business of creating. Under your feet
(legroom), above your head (headroom),
all around you the Volvo changes

into practical tractor, paves the way
for civilized commerce between recognized
nations. (Lack of recognition can be traced
to poor vision, seeing triple, three worlds

where there should be one.)
Trees behave like blades, falling and cutting
furrows at the same time. Plowed fields
await the migrants, the three-dimensional

ghosts haunting the supermarkets where squash
that sculpture parodies costs like art when
migrants hold their pennies to their eyes like
monocles and see no way to purchase. *Give*

credit where credit is due, spread the news, say
nothing when someone asks *what's happening?* Say
inflation when someone asks *what's up?* Say *fine*
when someone asks how you're doing but don't
reveal exactly how much you must pay as
result of migrant audit.

THE WARMTH OF HOT CHOCOLATE

Somebody told me I didn't exist even though he was
looking dead at me. He said that since I defied logic,
I wasn't real for reality is one of logic's definitions.
He said I was a contradiction in terms, that one side
of me cancelled out the other side leaving nothing.
His shaking knees were like polite maracas in the small
clicking they made. His moustache seemed a misplaced
smile. My compliments did not deter him from insisting
he conversed with an empty space since there was no
such thing as an angel who doesn't believe in God.
I showed him where my wings had been recently trimmed.
Everybody thinks they grow out of the back, some people
even assume shoulder blades are all that man has left
of past glory, but my wings actually grow from my scalp,
a heavy hair that stiffens for flight by the release
of chemical secretions activated whenever I jump off a
bridge. Many angels are discovered when people trying
to commit suicide ride and tame the air. I was just
such an accident. We're simply a different species,
not intrinsically holy, just intrinsically airborne.
Demons have practical reasons for not flying; it's too
hot in their home base to endure all the hair; besides,
the heat makes the chemicals boil away so demons plummet
when they jump and keep falling. Their home base isn't
solid. Demons fall perpetually, deeper and deeper into
evil until they reach a level where even to ascend is
to fall.

I think God covets my wings. He forgot to create some
for himself when he was forging himself out of pure thoughts
rambling through the universe on the backs of neutrons.
Pure thoughts were the original cowboys. I suggested
to God that he jump off a bridge to activate the wings
he was sure to have, you never forget yourself when you
divvy up the booty, but he didn't have enough faith that

his fall wouldn't be endless. I suggested that he did
in fact create wings for himself but had forgotten; his
first godly act had been performed a long time ago, afterall.

I don't believe in him; he's just a comfortable
acquaintance, a close associate with whom I can
be myself. To believe in him would place him in
the center of the universe when he's more secure
in the fringes, the farthest corner so that he
doesn't have to look over his shoulder to nab the
backstabbers who want promotions but are tired of
waiting for him to die and set in motion the natural
evolution. God doesn't want to evolve. Has been
against evolution from its creation. He doesn't
figure many possibilities are open to him. I think
he's wise to bide his time although he pales in the
moonlight to just a glow, just the warmth of hot
chocolate spreading through the body like a subcu-
taneous halo. But to trust him implicitly would
be a mistake for he then would not have to maintain
his worthiness to be God. Even the thinnest,
flyweight modicum of doubt gives God the necessity
to prove he's worthy of the implicit trust I can
never give because I protect him from corruption,
from the complacence that rises within him sometimes,
a shadowy ever-descending brother.

DWARF TOSSING

At least he's off the ground
although his name's the same: Sleepy,
Dopey, the five other aliases. I'm
not impressed by how many lift him, he's
lighter than air anyway, unfindable
till he puts on cologne.

In love with him now, tough guys do
the tough guy dance of assault
and battery. It begins like tango.
I'm small too, still fit in the palm
of a hand but only

God's. I've seen this before, war
movies, a grenade tossed at women's
known ineptness, a legal pass yet they
don't catch then make the touchdown, don't
want the hot potato, a black GI's

Saigon baby, it and guilt and whatever
else there is explode in their faces, an
extra point too many, the camel's, the dwarf's
broken back. I'd be a tall dwarf. I'd tower.
He doesn't, even when he's up there,
launched. He sees

the foam of his tosser's beer, thinks
ascension dwarfed the ocean; he must
become smaller than he ever was
to fit into the glass for splashdown, hero
home from aborted mission, moon
entirely missed, the flag still in his hand
still called *old glory* for lack of any new.

III

CONGREGATIONS

—for everybody that wanted me to get religion; I got something better.

Sunrise service and Rev. Jake is a dove, his wide
white robe that used to be our church, our tent back
when we had nothing but need of God spread like wings
and the only sermon necessary is his flight, the silk
fluttering as his preaching crescendos in a syncopated
verving of latinate reverence. White
transfigured feathers that motion blurs into one,
symbol of the trinity moving in and
out of each other like ghosts that are glare, afterglow,
memory of a fire, extinguishing tears that come
when we know we can't prolong burning.
St. Joan should still glow.
Just speaking of the glory made him faint.

Years later, his bible warms his hands, never
leaves them, a dialysis, transfusion that keeps him alive
in his retirement, behind the pulpit where he is
Pastor Dawes's shadow since Ethen Dawes as the source
of light has none, just his white bread robe shaking
crumbs like lint that hitchhike in the beams issuing
from his fingertips like Mandarin nails reminding
mostly women of sea coral, but in the light that way,
the lint, the crumbs are angel down we stuff our heads with,
pad our bras and fannies with, finish ourselves with.
Where's Jake Sardan in all this?

Waiting his turn as night vision must, trying
to be some sort of secret caravan en route to a mystic
place to verify reports of healing power, but wait
and see if that trip doesn't lead him to the same
pulpit where he window shops. A shadow, man all beard
you could say, the ominous we come to church to deny, to
be loosed from, the ominous that our perfume covers,

sweating all day in the basement kitchen, vanilla and
Creole spice (cayenne, file powder, a wish of garlic and leek)
rubbing on the musty armpits as if to marinate.

Look around at Sis. Elden's brim wider than the arms
of the crucifix but without promises; looking
into her eyes is impossible so what could be found
there must be sought elsewhere, Tahlma Ollet's
keyboard-wide bosom always in tune (can't tell
she most died bringing a no-count into the world) unlike
the old spinet whose keys look perfect but don't deliver
the notes, the pitches. Then they come; Tahlma Ollet
shouts, from kitchen below us, the sound coming up
through water pipes and plaster, thread-bare rugs that
the patting feet beat to death, a demon killing stomp;
through our own feet whose tapping is an African
distress call probably but we're out of range, out
of touch, although you can't tell from the way Tahlma's
shout comes on up through our root system then out
of our own mouths though we're out of range of the
pepper, out of touch with the onions she peels,
holding for a moment, before the knife enters,
a globe, a honeymoon, a cook's bible that she chops
into scriptures and makes us eat, tossing them
into every course: soup, entree, dessert.
Our shouting, our jubilation scares the ominous into
crouching behind our ribs where it intercepts what
would best serve us if it reached our hearts.

It does sometimes in the hint towards boogie-woogie
courtesy the tic in Elder Simpson's fingers, the
improvised pauses, hops, physiological product of
arthritis, spiritual product of faith, a holy rolling
of the eighty-eights when he plays *Sweet Home, 'Tis the
Old Ship of Zion.* Church starts to drift there,

crucifix, hand carved, painted brown, life-size becoming
mainstay, frame of the storefront ark serving Mt. Pleasant,
home of urban schools named for dead white presidents.

Ushers pass out bread slice shaped paper almost thick as
cardboard stapled onto tongue depressors, fans
from the House of Wills, funeral parlor, black owned
and operated—some might say death always was.
Not just grief shouts, not just fury rages.
Go, Willa, go; dance that holy dance, shake
those sinful tail feathers off! *Go on, Girl, shake
that thing; go on, Girl shake that thing!* Let God
have his way, let the spirit take control. Luther
Migby in the balcony with the wrong ideas for saving
and the right ideas for apropos fresh ways humming
Smoky Robinson, *you really got a hold on me.* One day
he'll redirect his lust, shout and taste the fruit
of Eden, won't have to eat again till
Wednesday Prayer Meeting, Thursday Tarry Service.
Friday reserved for the wakes.

Presenting: The House of Wills

Grand stucco walls, Italian villa in the slums, many
porticos, small windows—many exits for the soul that's
not supposed to be buried, not supposed to love the body
that much no matter how good a master the body's been.
Hough Avenue like a wide all-purpose arrow through the
heart, the spirit of the place. Hough Avenue like a skunk
pelt (they're pretty enough), like a gray stream through
the villa grounds, rhinestoned stream whose jewels lost
their lustre only, not identity; splendid underneath the
soot of sacrifice. *The House of Wills,* home of strength,
determination, finality, bodies dressed for their apocalyptic
meeting; nothing to do that day but get up, get moving,

get on board; that's what Elder Simpson's playing now; *there's*
a train a comin'; tilt the cross and it's a railway crossing
sign; *a train's a comin'* just like yesterday, simply
switching tracks, from underground to the sky; freedom
still the destination, hear the stationmaster call: Cleveland,
Ottawa, Heaven (that's right, *Heaven;* not New Haven anymore)—
don't get off too soon, don't slip.

No, never again into perditions, foul lovers
with the smell of a different woman on each finger, too
cheap to buy rings. I could name names but would rather
not spoil the enjoyment of Judgment.
Don't you just hate time for healing *all*
wounds? Some of the wreckage goes so far back
it's a candidate for carbon dating, select relics,
choice artifacts; I must depend, to outlaw nostalgic waxing
of the heinous, on cold facts like the Vietnam Vets black wall.
Even that cools my face when pressed against it like
a keepsake flower between the verses of Ecclesiastes.
A season for everything. A purpose. Names,
sour tastes, sweet tastes that still ache, rot
my teeth when I say them, tastes I just remember,
can't taste again, could barely swallow in the
first place; tastes that no longer satisfy, to which
my tongue is numb, immune, but still food.
Nothing can change that; still food
feeding something, substances something can live off
even if that thing shouldn't be fed. *Cause the bible*
tells me so.

Jake Sardan will probably shave his all gray head,
just ashes up there saying he's the bush extinguished,
God put out. Maybe he wouldn't burn after all, a
quick study who learns to eat fire and then learns
he can't go to heaven unless he can live off

something else, not the land either, heaven is
above that. Picture this: Jake Sardan, midway man,
running shell games at the county fair, every
once in a while belching up smoke that goes way up,
doesn't bother to come down among the sinners
except that something's wrong with this future
and with any other I can think of.

So go the other way, revert to frightening basics:
creation of the world. All this, every
damned (literally) thing there is came from that act.
We never can know what went wrong since there was no
deviation from a moment, when all was going right,
that didn't happen.

To now need a miracle makes no sense; that's what
got us started, keeps us going. Warm *Hallelujahs,*
lush *Amens,* the sedative of the congregation's
feet tapping the floors, a soft hammering, gentle
crucifixion. Nailed to the wall there's
no denying but just for a visible means of support.
Everything's eventually good for something. It
was the time that mine was the banner offering
Sunday school class. Miss Britt
whispered to me that God was watching so
do nothing I didn't want him to see. She
didn't mean this but I thought God was
giving me audience, that I was worth watching.
Self-esteem that wouldn't quit. Ticket
out of the ghetto. Sing *how I got over!*

LYNNE'S POEM: REASONS

1.

Because I don't drink
I see magic when pinkish wine goes into a glass
that is wide open (as a steeple should be, up there
in the best position to catch God and make him
come home where he belongs). Love that pink of

partial miracle, mild fever, the small raising
of temperature that must happen if one is not
aloof with life. It can happen
when you touch the terminated fetus
in which you find the fluttering
that confirms eternal presence. There are

even better ways to have it all, lean towards
a warm (as the fire ages past harm) stove
to hug like perfect father. Disappearance
can be redemptive; then we can't
see with our eyes, hear with our ears, touch
with our hands so will have to, at last, invent
new ways of being with someone, being ourselves,
being in the world.

2.

Because Lynne lifts spots from her vest, I admire
her. It's almost too delicious to bear, somebody
imparting elevation at such a moment,
that lifting, raising; that positioning of stain
for visitation—even if it won't come—by Grace.

Already the receptive are digging
where the moonshine and asafetida were
bottled, where Mandela walked out of Victor
Verster, where Dennis dreamt that dirt
by the shovelful would be elevated, a
stain that is the world.

NOTES

"Almost an Ode to the West Indian Manatee" is partially derived from a series of photographs by James Balog that appeared in the April, 1990 (vol. 177, no. 4) issue of NATIONAL GEOGRAPHIC.

Asafetida, a folk medicine or a spice popular in minute amounts in Indian cuisine, is derived from a foul-smelling weed of the same name as well as more descriptive names such as Devil's Dun or Stinking Gum. My parents both learned and practiced this remedy (for colds and flu mostly) in my father's native Cowan, Tennessee before bringing the health tradition north to Ohio. Although treatment perhaps more frequently consisted of solid, waxy chunks worn around the neck, my parents preferred a liquid version that they prepared themselves. The weed may be ground into spice as well though will likely be seldom used.

Kronos is a 1957 film featuring an electrified monster (whose body is a series of solid metallic gargantuan cubes and cylinders) from a planet presumably inhabited by other mobile transformers.

THE NATIONAL POETRY SERIES

The National Poetry Series was established in 1978 to ensure the publication of five books of poetry each year through a series of participating publishers. Each manuscript is selected by a poet of national reputation. Publication is funded by the Copernicus Society of America, James A. Michener, Edward J. Piszek, and The Lannan Foundation.

1990 PUBLICATIONS

Words For My Daughter, by John Balaban
Selected by W.S. Merwin. Copper Canyon Press.

Questions About Angels, by Billy Collins
Selected by Edward Hirsch. William Morrow & Co.

The Island Itself, by Roger Fanning
Selected by Michael Ryan. The Viking Press.

Rainbow Remnants in Rock Bottom Ghetto Sky, by Thylias Moss
Selected by Charles Simic. Persea Books.

The Surface, by Laura Mullen
Selected by C.K. Williams. University of Illinois Press.